Reign of Snakes

~

ALSO BY ROBERT WRIGLEY

In the Bank of Beautiful Sins
What My Father Believed
Moon in a Mason Jar
The Sinking of Clay City

Reign of Snakes

Poems by

ROBERT WRIGLEY

PENGUIN POETS

PENGUIN BOOKS
Published by the Penguin Group
Penguin Putnam Inc., 375 Hudson Street,
New York, New York 10014, U.S.A.
Penguin Books Ltd, 27 Wrights Lane,
London W8 5TZ, England
Penguin Books Australia Ltd, Ringwood,
Victoria, Australia
Penguin Books Canada Ltd, 10 Alcorn Avenue,
Toronto, Ontario, Canada M4V 3B2
Penguin Books (N.Z.) Ltd, 182–190 Wairau Road,
Auckland 10, New Zealand

Penguin Books Ltd, Registered Offices:
Harmondsworth, Middlesex, England

First published in Penguin Books 1999

10 9 8 7 6 5 4 3 2 1

Page ix contains an extension of this copyright page.

Library of Congress Cataloging-in-Publication Data
Wrigley, Robert, 1951–
Reign of snakes / by Robert Wrigley.
p.   cm.
ISBN 0 14 05.8919 8
I. Title.
PS3573.R58R45   1999
811'.54—dc21   98-48928

Printed in the United States of America
Set in Deepdene
Designed by Mia Risberg

for Philip, Jordan, & Jace

ACKNOWLEDGMENTS

These poems first appeared in the following publications:

Black Warrior Review: "Flies"; "Peace"
Crab Orchard Review: "Having Heard the Moon"; "Hoarfrost"
Five Points: "The Burned Cemetery"
The Georgia Review: "More Rain"
Gulf Coast: "Why Do the Crickets Sing?"
The Kenyon Review: "Conjure"; "Reign of Snakes"
The Missouri Review: "Art"; "Movies"; "Our Father";
    "Wanting God"
The Montserratt Review: "Prayer for the Winter"
Pivot: "Lessons"
Ploughshares: "Ice Fishing"
Poetry: "Dark Forest"; The Afterlife, Amazing Grace, Meditation at Bedrock
    Canyon, Night Music, and The Name, as "Earthly Meditations"
Poetry Northwest: "Bodies"; "Part Elegy"; "Sad Moose"
Quarterly West: "Open Grave"
Shenandoah: "Arrowhead"; "Nostalgia"; "The Pumpkin Tree"; "Prey"
Talking River Review: "After the Flood"

Thanks to Kim Barnes, Henry Carlile, Claire Davis, Dennis Held,
Ripley Hugo, Robert Coker Johnson, and Dorianne Laux, who read
many of these poems in draft and offered their guidance.

Gratitude as well to Edward Hirsch, Jane Hirshfield, Philip
Levine, and Dabney Stuart, for their help.

A special thanks to Golden Steele, master craftsman.

The author would like to express his gratitude
to the John Simon Guggenheim Memorial Foundation,
for its generous support during the writing of this book.

CONTENTS

Part Three

Part Four

Envoy

Beautiful my desire, and the place of my desire.
—Roethke

From this you see that—of necessity—
Love is the seed in you of every virtue
And of all acts deserving punishment.
—Dante

"Chrise," Nick said. "Geezus Chrise," he said happily.
—Hemingway

Part One

The Afterlife

1

Spring, and the first full crop of dandelions gone
to smoke, the lawn lumpish with goldfinches,
hunched in their fluffs, fattened by seed,
alight in the wind-bared peduncular forest.
Little bells, they loop and dive, bend
the delicate birch branches down.
I would enter the sky through the soil
myself, sing up the snail bowers
and go on the lam with the roots.
Licked by filaments, I would lie,
a billion love-mouths to suckle and feed.

Where the river will be next week,
a puddle two trout go savagely dying in.
Notice the bland, Darwinian sand: bone wrack
and tree skin, the ground down moon bowls
of mussels, viral stones dividing like mold.
At twelve, I buried the frog because it was dead
and dug it up because I'd been dreaming—
a fish belly light, a lowly chirruped chorus
of amens. I thought my nights might smell of hell.

Bland, humdrum, quotidian guilt—
if I've killed one frog, I've killed two.
Saint Rot and the sacraments of maggots:
knowing is humus and sustenance is sex.
It accrues and accrues, it stews
tumorous with delight. Tomorrow's
a shovelful, the spit of the cosmos, one day
the baby's breath is no longer a rose.

2

Dumb, would-be Siddhartha, I sat, lapped still
by the snowmelt rush. I was dull
as a beard and loved here
and there by mistake. The winter's last eagle lingered,
under its favored branch a garden
of delicate ribs. Air grew ripe
around them, like hands around
the heart of a prayer, the river a mirror
I was near believing: we are angels,
blue muck engenders a heaven,
this rush toward oblivion is the afterlife of all.

Somehow the frippery the cliff swallows sounded
escaped me. I could not imagine
the vaginal moistnesses of pleasure or birth.
That was the scream of a god, I thought,
but it was only tires on the highway above:
the beaver's spine dashed and rutted,
its belly-sides blown to bloody lips.
With brawny forelegs, it pulled itself my way,
blind to me, and tumbled down the rip rap
below the road. I wanted its yellow teeth—
it would not need them again—
so picked up a stone to smash its misery dead,
then heard the birds, their swirl and skirl,
their amorous warble in the fly-blown heights.

Festooned with their nests, the cliff
across the road looked mud-pocked. How the fissures held
and the nestlings clamored. How it goes
on and on—seed mash and the sun-blind
wings of goldfinches, swallows above

reproach, and a dying beaver writhing
on the rocks. Will my counsel have soothed it?
Did its soul come loose and lodge
in a sapling? I let fall the stone.
I sat. Where the marsh grass meets the sand,
where the wild rose kissed the season,
a hundred pink blossoms without a single want.

3

Plum and umber, dumb phlox spilling
from the canyon walls, its blue pinks deepened
each successive frost. An ancient rose,
a crone, sweet meat after meat for the bees.
The spirit dies a little, come spring,
each spring. Rib of trout, forgive me
my trespasses, forgive
my impatience with children, my curse
for the stinkbug and tick. I'm thinking
and thinking's a seed. The stillness
of the great blue heron is what I aspire to.
All the mud in this world is redolent
of just-cut meat, and nothing's at stake but the brain.

I am not the worst of my kind. There's succor
in that, though the beaver's gums are callused
as a ditch digger's hand and I am breaking
the laws of the state regarding game.
Slow as an hour hand the heron's leg
rises, the sun leans into its notch in the west.
My son calls from the cliff
across the river. From the drawn, distended petals
of his mother's body, he burst
into the world and began to mourn.
The spirit took root in his cry.

Why Do the Crickets Sing?

Because it is not enough to open the door
or sit on the porch, I have to go inside
the clamor the crickets send up
after a morning's long rain. I have to climb down
from the birdsong heights, let the water
wick my clothes cold and lick spit
salsify dabble my neck and eyelids with its kisses.

The nightcrawlers' earth musk makes me dizzy;
they lie spent and glistening in the light of the clouds.
Now the bells, the bells! The succulent hell boil
clamor of their wings, singing the hearts
of the one sun deep inside the seeds.
Let us open the mud book and pray.

Even the slug glister looms: perfect firmaments,
polestar and moon, only now
my eyes too focus on the blur of the bells,
fingertip whorls spin sudden into music.
It is like drowning, chorus and string,
a billion breath-moaned horns breaking like waves.

Taproot is thunder and moss is rain,
the drum of it what finally wakes me,
or brings me back from some brink,
some light that held me down to pull me up:
or else it is the kettledrum rumble of the field mouse—
a shriek of terror, soar of the hawk descending.

Dark Forest

. . . and then, in dreaming,
The clouds methought would open and show riches
Ready to drop upon me, that, when I waked,
I cried to dream again.
                                        —Caliban

I love the way the woods arrange themselves
for my convenience: here's the stob

I hang my pants on and here
the shrub I nestle my still-warm

underwear over, out of each leg hole
a leaf like an almond eye, one black

fly strolling the vent like a big city boardwalk.
And see how my shirt flung up

is the residue of flame,
a long smoke fading in the weeds.

I hear my boots go running,
though they will not go far down that ravine:

they miss my socks, one fist-sized stone
in the toes and thrown.

I'm ready now, dark forest.
Bring on your snakes and bears,

your coyotes singing praises
to my pink and almost hairless flanks.

*

Bring on the icy night, the cocktail stars,
the flamboyant, androgynous sun going down.

Let my soles go bloody
through the puncture weeds and shards,

let my legs be slashed by thorns:
I will follow my old compass, slouching

toward the north. I will paint myself
in the mud wallows of elk and make my skin

a new brown thing. Give my eyes to the ravens,
my heart to the ungainly buzzard, its head

gone red over all the earth's
uncountable cadavers, liberator of the dust.

I bequeath my clothes to the unraveling jays
and I will, if I should survive the night,

rise reborn, my opposable thumbs
surrendered to the palms, to find

in a snowmelt puddle a draught
of the same old wretched light,

seeing as the water stills at last
the man I refuse to be.

Hoarfrost

This morning the swing set's a confection,
even its chains flocked thick
as crustless loaves, the painted steel frame
diaphanous with light but gargantuan.
Lace of ice, vapor blades,
the heat of my one gloved hand
would ease you back to water,
and there, where the plain tubular rung
supports the spraddled legs, a dangling
growth I breathe on
to clarify, to half-thaw and see inside.
It's a small bird, a sparrow, I think,
frozen by its foot and swaddled in a headdress
of flightless feathers—a little chief,
a venerable elder, savior of the tribe of winter.
But no, it's just a bird, gray and indistinct,
winter-killed but statistically irrelevant,
though I see now through the fading,
breathed-away frost its eyes were open
when it died. It might have been
like flight then, the last feeble
electric spasm in its brain seeing
the earth turned over from the air.
What wings there, in the final dream light
of a dying bird. What a vista,
as the sun went down and it soared
into the vast, geometrical whiteness
of ice.

Flies

They come from the walls, from the house
logs stacked green and cracked along the grain,
from the gapped, inadequate joinery,
from their lairs to ours, from the larval slops
at the mild outer edges of the compost pile.
Wings pure plasticine and calcite
veined black, they back in
toward the very rot they came from,
until, by midwinter, the unused troughs
where the windows slide are furrows
of that glad disassembly—black shards
of carapace and thorax, whole heads
and whole heads of hairlike legs.
For now, however, late fall, they remain aloft,
battering their eye-faceted, boneless skulls
against glass or spinning periodic and dervish
on sills, floors, desks, and tables,
a million living jewels enacting
the curse of a god or an unearthed pharaoh.
I go room to room, sweeping them up
with a broom and pan, or pulling them off
with the long wand of the vacuum, sometimes
still aspin, sometimes still flying,
a hill of them daily accruing, dark
with shimmers, a confetti of husks in the shop vac,
a wing-shatter lace I will remember come spring
and dump atop the thinning snow
mounded over last year's leaves—the leaves
I have yet to rake, the snow that has not yet
fallen, the flies, like this one,
just a moment ago come down before me,

dazzled by the sheer, impossible blankness,
against which, until the end,
we must work.

Sad Moose

He's shed his left horn and lists
to the right, working the last one
hard against trees and stones.
An old bull, his dewlap's shot
with silver, his winter hide
shelving off like crumbling shale.
High on the brisket there's a wound,
oozing and festered, the fletched end
of an arrow worn down but still visible.

He's carrion on the hoof. There's a bear
nearby, I'll bet, or a lion.
The howls of last night's coyotes loom
explanatory today, one pack's in line,
and another is on the way.
Though half the pond is iced over,
the bottom's algae, new mosses,
and some translucent shoots
of the earliest aquatic weeds.

Besides, isn't the oar
above the right ear lighter in water?
Each day for a week I've watched him,
the ribs defined into claws,
a slow strangulation in his own
stout bones. "Stout bones," I say,
aloud, and the submerged head
comes up dripping, an arc splash
flung by the antler.

In two tremendous leaps, he's battering
the brush between us, and I'm

shinning up a lodgepole no bigger
than my thigh, pulse pounding
counterpoint to his moosely abandon.
Ten yards of deadfall and alder
and he's still. I'm slung among
squirrel perches and looking down
at forty-five degrees into his eye.

It's the upward eye, the extant
horn on edge, down against a fallen snag
like a kickstand. He's a pentapod,
the eye from this angle
blue-black and cloudy, like motor oil
laced with milk. Five more minutes
and he's back in the water
and I'm down, picking my quiet way
through duff and dead branches to the trail.

This morning when I left the cabin,
I considered the pistol there.
In my jacket pocket, five bullets
rattle like beads. Fire, I think,
and language, possibly love.
I have these things a moose does not.
Sad moose, sad man. Sad is the world
a while, as it waits to feed,
some of us seed and tendril, some of us stone.

Part Elegy

Somewhere in this half-wild canyon, not far
I don't suppose from where I sit, my old cat's fur,
strawberry blond and fine as chinchilla,
riffles in the breeze, though his eyes
are glazed over or gone. In his fourteen years
he'd lived in eight houses, in three states;
been gnawed on twice by dogs, by some
cruel canine irony Black Labs both times, the very breed
we would buy the year he turned ten,
the summer after he'd tangled with a coon,
the summer before a neighbor boy
blew his leg to boney smithers with a BB gun.
Long-haired, a dust mop of thistles and burrs,
he would come to me sometimes,
reluctantly, a yard-long limb of thorns
knotted between his hind legs, his voice
rusty iron but authoritative, and he'd allow himself
to be turned on his back, allow my hands
that matty unweaving, allow the wet rasp
to spin in his throat. Yesterday
the neighbors' dog treed a bear,
and I remembered the tut-tutting real estate
saleswoman in Oregon saying *That's a cat*
who should sleep on a velvet pillow, and she was
part right. He sat on the woodpile,
his winter coat plumped out huge and smooth,
mane and cowl swept elegantly back
by the breeze. And just minutes ago,
last day of the second week of his absence,
I heard a clatter of paws across the porch
and still looked up hopeful. It was a wild procession:

our younger cat, Sam, chased by a lanky Siamese
I'd never seen before, who was in turn
chased by the dog.
                        Then they stopped.
No whirl of limbs and fur, no growl or bark,
just two cats and a dog, standing
in a perfect parabola, a congregation
at the axis of which sat, placidly, a mouse,
one jewel of blood gleaming on his right ear.
Someone could tell me now, I'm sure of it,
sparing no detail of musculature
and no behavioral insight, someone could say
how, kinesiologically-speaking, that mouse
let us all know he knew
the odds, the score, the food-chain declensions
that had left him head-bloodied
and doomed to die. The thing is,
there was a camera on the shelf
just behind me. I could have caught it all,
the four of them, that quivering, attenuated stasis
through which none of them moved. I should have,
I suppose, but rose instead
and went to the door and shooed the dog
and both cats away and crouched there
alongside that mouse. "Run," I said,
but it only sat, whiskers not quite moving.
Now I could see its other wounds,
bloodless punctures over the shoulders and neck,
the left forepaw held up, dog-style.
When I picked it up by the tail
it squirmed then quieted, dangling
just above my waist all the way down
the driveway and the dusty road
to the mailbox, to where the last
hopeful trickle of the creek still murmured.

And there I set it loose, having to poke at it repeatedly
until it moved, wobbly and uncertain,
among the weeds and the year's last water,
into a landscape grown daily more cold,
where his kind, still in hunger and in need,
might yet live.

Art

How the buck could have tangled himself
so tightly in a three-strand fence
was anyone's guess, each wire
torqued in a knot of barbs his legs, neck,
and new velveted horns were at the heart of.
He must have hit it full tilt in the dark,
momentum spinning him through
and in, every thrash thereafter
sawing flesh, by the time I arrived,
just past dawn, sawing deeper than bone.

From a hundred yards up the fence line
I could see his still occasional spasm.
The staples sung in the still air then
like lunatic clarinets.
There was nothing to think about here,
not for any of us. I was miles from home
and empty-handed, my pocketknife too dull
and small to cut his throat, and anyway, the way
he pitched and fought as I approached
might have left me dead before him.

I will call it a vigil then. I stayed and waited
until he died. At first the dog could not abide
the place and danced and whimpered
then found a pheasant's trail to follow.
I moved to where his one remaining eye
might see me and sat on a rock
among the new spring flowers and grassy fodder.
Soon he settled into the process, and the flies
embossed his bloody hide, and bile
frothed from the corner of his mouth, and he died.

*

Old man Behring, who owns the land,
notched the skull plate out with a bow saw
and sold the toe-head rack to the horn collector
in Reubens. Coyotes strung the guts
in a smorgasbord of coils and organs,
worried the haunches to bitten-out hulks.
And today, October 1, 1996, six months' weather
and the good work of magpies and maggots
have made this display, this sculpture, this door
the wind leans against, and one day, will open.

Having Heard the Moon
Is No Longer Desirable in Poetry

—for James Hart

I for one am relieved, although I understand
        they mean the ordinary, maudlin moon, stone

that's launched a thousand verses, waxed full.
        Flagrant symbol, no smoke of city lights

to veil its scars, it has nothing left to flaunt here
        but the way it looks at us when it thinks we're gone,

when it's blind to our long, blue gaze.
        As it rises in the notch between two mountains,

it shows a skeletal tree invisible from where I sit
        any other time of night or day, the bent trunk and pair

of curved limbs no less a dancer than a sculpted ton of bronze.
        A blade of light knifes the lake's black surface,

and the way it aligns itself with the trail back to camp
        is convenient, or lucky, that's all, even though

that one straight stretch across a treeless slope of quartz
        is like walking into the blossom of a just-struck match.

Everywhere crystals shoot light in flickers and shafts, and I
        am the pink and shimmering flaw inside a jewel.

Open Grave

This wedge of county land shows up
every year on the tax bill. "Cemetery,"
it says, "$4.00." I'd guess I'm a double sawbuck
into the place by now, though an actuary might say more.
The view from Ida Hume's tombstone:
a mile of silver river down a rock
and timbered canyon, postcard perfect,
even the other way, across the gravel road
the one-room schoolhouse turned hay barn,
in the slanted cupola a redtail hawk,
feathered clapper in the pure bell of air.

On the plot next door, a clutch
of artificial flowers faded neutral in the sun,
then a tarped-over mound of fine, black earth,
and next to it the open grave
I squat at the edge of, considering.
Even now, high noon, all four
corners lit up, the hole breathes
a cool draft upward. A shovel's inside,
and a pair of pre-cut, template sticks—
one for depth and one for width.
There's digging to be done before the vault.

Truly, Ida Hume, this is a fine place
to be planted, though what grass there is
is coarse and clumped, the whole mown place
mostly knapweed and thistle. And what moves me
to hoist myself up and drop down
into a stranger's fresh grave, I can't say
for sure, though I notice,

on my back like this, that the sky
through the turf's rectangular lens is a blue
to make you weep, almost painful,
and much harder, the climb back out.

Part Two

Amazing Grace

1

Tick-tick, the clicks of the paper wasps
whispering at the window: I'm allured
and cured by the sun; I enter the light
celestial, my night cloak flares into smoke.
Silken travails, the day is knee-deep
in the transits of spiders, every weatherward surface
dappled by sacs—the pine in a winding sheet,
the broad-shouldered barn in a negligee.
That hornet's nest aquiver in the eaves, tissue
and comb, a comely, mournful hillbilly hymn.
My dream-sleeves ravel, my navel winks,
I am present at the advent of an hourglass of blood.

Here's mud in your I, gentle dreamer,
the firmament's flagrante delicto, all the knuckles
of snails spilling their postulant prints,
hills made thighs in the day moon's boudoir.
The ardent prey, clutching his flowers,
a gentleman caller done up like a ghost,
bound for the lick of the cows and the does.
The days are shorter and the nights are cold.
I sneer at the wasps' hysteria. The nest breast
wobbles in the westerly wind, the day
is a grave, its eight black legs atotter under the pall.

My dust, my yawp, my top-heavy blossom!
There's pollen on this stamen still, the sun
is warp, the earth is woof, my tusk's a tooth
I grow light-headed in the presence of.
Between the bull's mighty horns, the lacemaker's

done her work quite well, spinnerets radiant
and a dozen flies like whole notes
in a twisted scale, a rondeau. Ruminant
under such music, we believe we believe in the end.

2

These gray, nameless beetles, passing miraculously
through walls: the whisk of a swatter's no balm,
the ceiling's freckled with their stews.
And where does the sumac get off,
gone bloody down the slopes, late leaves
nearly black, like teardrops of liver
in the golden, autumn grass?
My hair's blown back, my eyes are tearing,
the winds of the calendar snarl and bite.
I've got half a mind to think with
the worms. Rain's their affliction,
and we're here gasping in an arid year.

Only everywhere the bugs are reeling.
Last night I killed a cricket
with a glance: the cats have learned
to study the web-work of my eyes,
though not the youngest tom—all tumble and sprawl,
a sleepy rumble, a fish breath wretch,
like me. There's no blood husk in the ashtray,
that's a ladybug sucking some inks; the eyes
on the Io moth's wings don't blink
but weep. Where there's fire there's talc and dust.
The parchment nest wobbles like an udder.

I know these dreams are a ruse,
a camouflage, a trick of the eye.

The deathwatches click at my windows,
and weather undoes their orbicular book.
The egg comb inside is barren. Petal dumb,
I blunder, a dull, unseasonable sun sets
the roof to ticking too. The whine of insects flying,
a kind of ooze in the air, the sigh
of the body's low flight, something peering
from the hatches like a child, into the caustic sky.

3

Sweet Charlotte of the imperfections, that pig
is a groin on legs, a land mass of meat.
Say the man in the man is no longer
than a thumb, a cross section sealed in aspic,
head cheese of the head cheese, salt rime
in a hat, the pathos of an onion peeled.
I put on Arachne's prideful cloak. Not
a bad fit, all the gods in their venal dances:
I've skinned a snake, I've crushed a spider—
thank the wind for worser curses.

And isn't this some rube tangle in the end?
A rush of flesh the spider clothes, the night
before the first hard frost. Rise up,
mostly dead, note the filaments of liquid silk
in your first three-minute egg, spittle thin,
albuminate, noosing the fat blood bottle
of the timely heart. And there, scuttling out of cover,
the fiddleback arachnid sees its shadow:
it's like a dream, the first dream. Dark
beyond the confines of the skin shell, a thin, translucent twin,
walking on air.

The Pumpkin Tree

Up a lattice of sumac and into the spars
of the elderberry, the pumpkin vine had climbed,
and a week after first frost
great pendulous melons dangled like gods
among the bunches of lesser berries
and the dazzled, half-drunken birds.

Then the pumpkins fell, one by one, each mythical fruit's
dried umbilicus giving way in a rush
of gold and a snow of elliptical leaves.
A skull thud, the dull thunk of rupture,
a thin smoke then, like a soul, like dust.

But the last, high up and lodged
in a palm of limbs and pithy branches,
sways now in the slightest breeze and freeze
after freeze caves in on itself
and will, by spring, cast its black

leathery gaze out over the garden
like the mummy of a saint or an infirm
and desiccated pope. Below, where the others fell,
that seed not eaten by winter birds,
one, say, buried in meat and a sheath

of skin, will rise. From its blunt,
translucent nubbin, a leaf trifoliate
and a stalk as succulent as bamboo, it will climb
blithe as a baby Christ up the knees
of the wood it cannot know it is bound for.

Lessons

The water is cold, and I cling to the side
of the pool like a primitive, a film
some caustic cleanser might remove.
Now and then I leave and pad wetly out
and shiver at the chain-link fence
my mother sits outside of.
Six or seven, I had clung to her
and thought nothing of it,
that first day she'd hauled me with my sister
into the girls' locker room,
and oblivious I'd stripped to laughter and screams,
my boy's dull pud, a pink finger, pointing nowhere.
I was ashamed then and now my mother is too,
because she tells me, the only child there
not splashing and laughing, her lips so close
to the chain-link diamonds I can feel
her hissed breath warm my ear,
and that seems enough,
so I rise and go back
and enter the water
the way a woman, I'm told,
might give herself to a man she does not love.

Movies

On the move again, the kidney stone,
      rough as a barnacle chiseled off a pier,
brought me to my knees
      before the video store's cool return slot.
I slid the cassette inside,
      waved to the frightened clerk,
and saw how clearly the sun winked once
      from the dangling keys in his hand.
My forehead made a smeared, translucent flower
      on the window glass, my breakfast
brought color to the sidewalk grit.

All the way to town I'd hung myself
      across the steering wheel and sung
along in a cold sweat
      to the golden oldies station: "I feel
good, I knew that I would,"
      that famous verse from the book of Job,
in the exquisite James Brown translation.
      By noon, I was anesthetized
and plumbed, coming to in a blue
      institutional room, where the kindly nun
I'd once been neighbor to prayed
      for my complete and swift recovery.

And here was the abashed and burly urologist,
      sheepish, no jagged, infinitesimal pearl
in his paw, in a funk,
      my urinary tract spelunking having netted him nothing.
Now from the hall an internist's voice
      demanding morphine, and my hand,

the IV having blown out its vein,
   fat as a ball glove and foreign at my wrist.
So where are the boils and scabs? I think,
   and could that hirsute phlebotomist
truly be the star of last night's film?

The cook, the thief, his wife, and her lover.
   Consider the labor costs saved
for me here, the self-administering
   Demerol pump clicking in my hand
like castanets. O, sweet sisters
   of the Carondelet, tsk-tsking,
I am taking the Lord's name in pain,
   in vain, as the hospital's new wing rises
to the accompaniment of jackhammers
   on my skull. That's Captain America
revving his hog across the hall,
   or just a flag, flaccid in the sterile air.

I could be Bogart's Rick, bidding
   the perfect Ingrid Bergman of my healthy body
good-bye. There's nothing on TV,
   but it's in color. And when I pee
that first post-op time, the stainless steel
   urinal warming in my hand's no miracle
at all: I've been drinking fire,
   I seem to have swallowed a sword.
And it dawns on me, as they gather near
   my bed—the nurse, the surgeon

in his tennis togs and lab coat,
   the grim, defensive urologist—that
that is Bogart on the screen, damned
   near dead, peeling leeches from his legs
and comforting Katharine Hepburn.

"Wait a second," I say, and everyone moves
from the foot of the bed to the head,
         even the pink and lovely candy-striper,
holding out my lunch of Jell-O, broth,
         and ginger ale. I need a shave,
I'm greased with sweat. She swings
         the table across me. No one else can see her.
She pats my hand, and her voice,
         running the gamut of emotions
from A to B, assures me,
         I'm looking better all the time.

The Theory and Practice of Fables

Bagworms gilded the ornamental yews either side
of the front porch, and the boy was employed
one long summer day, plucking whole buckets loose—
rough and supple, conical pods
in their needlework of brown coniferous silks.
And the fire they made made him
what, exactly? A kind of demon or god
at his desultory chores, stirring
the smoky dome of them, the whistles and pops
as their juices boiled boring him too,
even the fat granddaddy teed up top.

Through shawls of smoky satin it opened,
vaginate, he might have thought,
or like the neighbor bulldog's cock unsheathed,
an angry, bloody limb and wound.
It rose a full long, terrible inch,
its never-wings yawing out once, like elbows,
when it blew, and the goo of it,
the gummed yew-mouthings hot as solder
blistered his cheek in a pestilential kiss and shriek.

See how they go, slow
and hard, swift and fearful, the fabulous
tortoise and hare are running, edible each,
mythically rich, pure meat for the teller of the larger tale,
who rests his face, moon-pocked and carbuncular with warts,
on his fist, then tips the quill, the ashen stick,
the nib of gold just once against his tongue
and begins.

The Knowing

And what rough beast is this? Adam asked.
He'd already named the others and had welcomed the woman,
Eve, as only he could. There was no one else.

It was there in the air between them, its snarl
in the salts of their mingled sweat, its pummel and purr,
its bloody jaws, the bliss of its bottomless predatory eyes.

It made the air a mirror, a second earth, the garden
of meaning and desire: here was her hip in the sway of a flower.
There were no ghosts; there was nothing else to call it yet.

And it was like a child, but there were no children then,
no kiss, no rose, no rage, no stone.
And yet, here it was, resembling some face that was his,

some space that was nowhere without her, the woman,
Eve, beholding it too. Tender, beckoning,
it would cost them this paradise and more.

After the Flood

These are the halcyon days
of heavy equipment, the back-up beeps
from bulldozers and dump trucks
more common than birdsong, the air,
my wife maintains, so redolent
of testosterone a deep breath
could bring on a beard. Yesterday
we watched two men in a motorboat
salvage lumber from a back-eddy pool.
The river boiled beneath them,
treacherous with dead-heads and flotsam.
Neither man wore a life jacket
of course. We'd spread a blanket
under a tree, the kids collected ladybugs
for the garden. I wanted to kiss her neck,
her shoulders bare in the sun for the first time
in months. Your age, she said, or younger.
I reconsidered my cigar. By now
they must have had enough
lumber to frame a small house
or a barn—two-by-sixes, two-by-eights,
straight-grained fir and pine, no common
yard stuff, only select. Imagine
starting over, she said. A gable floated by,
a tatter of black tarpaper trailing.
For a moment, I was a hole in the air,
like the shape of a house
where a house had been, or a room—
a bedroom after love, the kitchen
by meal light and laughter.
Everything gone, she said.

And it was, the scrape and beep of roadwork,
the furtive, early bird songs,
even the calls of the children
at another vivid hatch of bugs.
I was falling into the light, I think, I was
swallowed by silence, when the line came,
the outboard whine driving men
and wood upstream, and one man—
bless his fool heart and mine—
waved his cap at us and whooped.
They had all they could carry
this load. They'd be back
to begin again. I rose
from where I lay and nuzzled her neck.
She laughed and shrunk from the itch
of my whiskers, then turned
and kissed me back.

The Burned Cemetery

Understand the years of drought, the vast expanse
of unused land next door, labor costs,
the bottle rocket some local kid let fly.
After all, the dead were beneath it,
or above, safe in any case, no matter what
your ecclesiastical stance. And anyway,
the fireline the bulldozer cut around the place held.
All in all, it wasn't the worst land to burn.

And those of us who followed the smoke,
whose houses squat nearby, surrounded by tinder and fuel,
have little to do now but take it all in—
the two plush yews turned blackened racks, each
limb tip gray and soft as the untapped ash of cigarettes;
the occasional knot of artificial flowers
still bubbling in the shade of their scorched stones;
the resident field mice thrashing.

By night, under the bright full moon,
it is a landscape Goya might love, a negative,
a photograph snapped mid-rapture—every smoke wisp
a soul, every char mark on marble a flame,
and the whole blank expanse of grass
and weeds the night sky turned upside down.
You can walk among the stars where no one lives.
You could fall headlong to the roots on fire.

Wanting God

Even if I were not so drunk, but merely sick
at heart, lost among the littered streets
my life resembles, the lock on this church door
would still offend me. I've been drinking
the blood of that lesser savior, *Vitus*
Lambrusca: unsanctified,
it still goes hard to my head.

Even the pigeons in the belfry find shelter
from the rain, but then they have no hands
and would not lift a hymnal nor a gilded candelabrum
with a mind to the pawn.
Just loftier knaves they are, cut off
from the sacristy the same as me,
and the holy water font we both might sip from.

For I confess, I thirst, and the rain
tonight is vinegar. How in the world did I get here,
halfway home and sore afraid?
The pigeons themselves are bells,
a carillon of coos, and their pews
are curbs and gutters, and the alley cats are Satan.

Let me tell you, Officer, I have been blinded
by the beam of your light, but now I see.
If I could just find my way, I would lose myself
in a new kind of prayer, considering
for example the assembly of God
and my lack of useful tools.
I see to the left of your riot gun
there's Jesus on the dashboard, where the miraculous radio

cracks and commands, where the various radars
spread out their invisible robes.

Here is my house, yes, bless you,
thank you for the ride. The sharp rap
of your nightstick on the door
will surely wake my wife. And look,
there is the streetlight
I sometimes watch for hours on end
this time of night. Don't you love the way the bats
come fluttering there, weaving after moths?
There is no way we will ever enter
the darkness and believe like they do.

Some of those bugs—the midges and millers—
we can hardly conjure up in the light,
but above us, in the black grid
of night and electrical wires,
they are found and found,
and the bats fill themselves full
in the vast faithless vault that we,
with our keys and lights, would like to believe
we too shall enter.

Our Father

A hand, or the shadow of a hand,
passes over. The wind, you'd think,
or the way some sad, benevolent god
might stroke the hovering raven,
of all creation his favorite jewel.

So now the hollyhocks shake their hankies
and the dog looks up, abased
by domestication, while the minions
of aridity suffer their thorns and scales,
singing world without love, amen.

You'd think the raven's rosiny squawk
was complaint, an oiled curmudgeonly bell.
You'd think a decent god would
allow a man to love another man.
You'd think there was no place like hell

but earth, awash in its armies
and damned to believe in nothing
so much as dollars and death, the economies
of raven and of man—one who flies,
one who tries and tries to pray.

Part Three

Meditation at Bedrock Canyon

1

Unloved, unlovely, the bull thistle slouches
in the fields these days. It spills
its seedy tears and, shrunken, gallumphs,
a dessicate dump the strumpet sparrows
spread far and wide. I'd die for an eye
like that, horse-sized and purple as a bruise.
I would lose the light and shake every shadow,
let the droop of my skin go
tacking the map. Oars of a boat,
my hands cup the musical waters,
the morning star sets sail in a spindrift of seeds.

What bird is that? The word
is the measure, the tongue
is the string, the flying change
of the elk, his majestic horns,
the delicate purple embouchure of his muzzle—
buss of blossom, thistle kiss. His piss
is rank as a composted heart.
How do the autumn bees dance
such desperate fandangos? The smoke
from a burn of stubble deranges their eyes,
and all pollen's past its innocuous prime—
stickum of whiskey, saffron booze.

That buzz is the muscular gizzard's grind.
Gray of the sky mocks
the pheasant's tongue. I've sung my seminal song
and dreamed the earth herself took note,
my muse of dirt, my mole hole umbilicus

to the dark. All the best songs
and symphonies blow the candles out,
there's a measure in the clef
of the skin and the lips. I'm a weed
and a weevil, a wing and an arc.
Any where I hang on is a home.

2

Friable loam alitter, the bulge
of the burrow's entry shaft, the uneasy maw
it makes, obscene, its badger come forth
snarling, some black secretion of primordial rage.
This is the forest medieval, stump plundered
and birthed by a hag, the swagger
of resource consultants festered in its slash.
Here the long rebuilding takes place:
blackberry scaffolds and the footings of stone,
a coyote's just-so scatter of bones,
probable gallows of a weathered snag.

That pair of ravens wobbling there—
Caliban and Caliban—they're drunk on fermented light.
They say I take my scars too seriously.
It's my Roman nose, my stupid clothes—
what's a mink without his fur?
I'll pass on skin I cannot kiss
and blow a thousand bubbles, little bobs,
along the stream. Who's minding the nest,
you beasty birds, what fledglings fail
by your profligate caws?
White as fluff, your shadows, cock and hen.

And the wren, aggressively puckish, preens,
its perch the dead elk's rack of horns.

All are punished, and punished for love,
the first human wonder of the world.
Bloodroot, tumeric, bladderwort, puccoon—
call it what you will but bow
to its flower. The stigma, the anther, the sepal, the stem.
The day's eyes nod in a cool wind.
They are blind from the root hairs up.

3

The haunch of the fallen bull, worried
by a badger, twitches
from this distance. Brain weave
of a bramble obscures the tug and smack.
What new sacrilege is this, Walt Disney?
Where are the Hottentot lions?
the Yiddish cats? What language speaks
that widowed cow across the way,
mouthing down the last supple bloom in sight?
She stayed for the purple, she mourneth not,
I've reentered my clothes like a story.

Slump, dump, the green world sags.
I wish I could photosynthesize.
Summer's dark contusions—scab of knee
and plowed field, the peeled back skids
of landed logs: I sing a song
of loss across the sky.
I am myself and nothing else.
I'd welcome the sky in my branches.
From a night's long gulf of sleep,
my daughter unfolds and holds
all the light there is before her, and I am new,
the dew come down with its kiss.

Reign of Snakes

1. *Revival*

During the heat of summer days, they sprawl
in the shade of sumac glades
or hunt the bottom-watered thickets—buck brush
and blackberry—dining on mice.
And beneath every yellow pine for miles,
the scaly, pulse-quickening sticks
from each tree's unlimbing.
At dawn and dusk you can find the snakes
on rock face shelves, basking,
sun still funneling up from basalt.
There are side canyon gullies, drywashes
and scumbled slides, half stone,
half soil, and shed skins blow in them
like a snow of translucent leaves,
while deep inside the winter chambers, a boil
of approximate sleep, lidless eyes
unseeing, a fist of snakes as big as a man.
I stopped one night, road-drunk,
at the torch-lit revival tent
of a trinity of back woods preachers,
in Arkansas or the boot heel of Missouri,
where a graying, hortatory praisemaster sang hymns
of joy, and his stern wife damned us all
to fire. I rose to leave, filled with free ice tea,
a fistful of tracts in my hand,
then stopped, as the pale, thin son
held the snake above his head and began to dance,
the rattler grasped mid-length
in his left hand, the right

stroking the jeweled scales, a caress,
as he brought the head to his lips,
his eyes sublimely closed.

2. Confession

As a boy I flogged a corn snake to death
with the limber end of a leaf rake.
It took a while, but I let my friends help,
and once, leaping crossways
onto the backyard hammock,
my head hung over the edge,
I saw the copperhead upside down
at the end of the ground's rush by.
Massive and beautiful, tucked among
hummocks of crabgrass
at the edge of a scar of clay,
it stayed there, tasting the air above,
then oozed away, machine of muscle,
machine of oil and bone.
And I have hacked rattlesnakes to bloody hunks,
grunting my rage, and made with a single surgical blow
a guillotine of the shovel's edge.
I have skinned them out
and exhumed the damp, ruffled carcass of a mouse.
And once, I followed the aim
of my grandfather's cane to see one,
a blacksnake high on the scaly bark
of a cemetery silver maple,
a sign, he told me, of evil buried near.
My grandfather knew every corpse around us alive,
but wouldn't say which it might have been,
only tapped his pipe empty
against the shining, ostentatious obelisk

of the man who owned the mine he'd worked in,
then plucked a carnation for his lapel.

3. The Fall

Why snakes? Always snakes?
Why that long narrow room, nearly dark,
"Snake's Uptown Pool Hall and Tattoo Parlor,"
its phosphorescent fixtures shedding
a skin of light, half a dozen rectangular lily pads
fading down a swamp. Why Snake himself?
Buddha-fat, he sat behind the counter
dispensing chalk and balls,
and when summer's dank heat came down
he glowered in the exhalations of his oscillating fan,
naked to the waist—chest, back, and arms
a cathedral expanse of tattoos: twenty or more
curvaceous women wearing nothing
but strategically placed snakes.
My eyes adjusted to the dark,
but to little else. Already my friends
were gone, whooping their bikes down the back streets
and laughing. Blue portals in the half light,
my pupils must have loomed above my lips,
and the hiss I could not stop making, the long slithering
ess that was to have been my ruse and request—
a Slim Jim, a soda—now sputtered out
into a nest of breasts and scales, an evil I entered
saying less than a word. Snake looked down.
"You like my serpents, boy?" he asked,
and it would have been as though he'd said it
to the light, the door's wash flashbulb fast,
a hot crack of balls giving chase,
the fat man's dry hack of laughter behind me.

4. Catechism

"You want to taste what's good, you got to lick
what's evil," he tells me. Call it theology,
catechism, Guiseppe "Big Joe" Truccano's
weekly hour of prayer for poontang
and heavy tips. His tie's unbowed,
a monogrammed handkerchief
covers his ruffled shirt and cummerbund:
he's the handsomest man in the world,
tends bar in the city at Anthony's slick club,
and claims the men's room attendant there
unzips his fly for him and fishes out his cock
with a spoon. I'm enthralled. We're at Toon's Bar & Grill,
it's nine a.m., and all the Sunday air's
a battle of dueling church bells.
I've skipped the service to be here,
for the communion of boot black coffee,
the host of a day-old doughnut, glazed.
Big Joe's got an illegal Bloody Mary, envy
of the half dozen jittery alcoholics around us.
He's got a platter of hash browns and pan gravy,
two over easy eggs and two strips of bacon
arranged on top like an edible crossbones and skull.
"Mama believed I'd be a priest," he says, "and I swear
to you, Junior, I believe I am.
I go down," he tells me, "every week I go down
on my knees and do the penance
the sin-shifter says I should"—
then the switchblade, sprung out
to hash his eggs and bacon in the spuds.
It's spring, the earth's salacious remains are rising.
Under the spell of his eyes the lewdest robins

are treacle, the long disquisitions
on feminine anatomy more beautiful than roses.
Outside, the last quiet moments
on the street, before the churches empty.
I have a minute, maybe two, to make it back
but I don't move. "Go on," he says,
and as I rise to leave he pulls the handkerchief
from his collar, and drags out the medal
of St. Christopher too, size of a quarter
on a silver chain he quickly stuffs back in.
It'll be all they have for a partial ID
months later, the pewter melted
under a blowtorch blast, the Saint's elongated
robes oozing down to the sternum, the Child unscathed
atop the flow, and Big Joe—armless, legless,
battered, even the genitals gone—
unfound for weeks in the tall grass
of some abandoned orchard, beneath a barren tree.

5. *Fellowship*

The men who made the railroad bed,
hauling off the overlay of rock and soil,
who laid the ties and rails, those men
suffered their wages and more,
now and then the great diesel shovel
unloading with a two ton bite
a hundred pounds of rattlesnakes
from a den, thudding on the dump truck
roofs and hoods like a scattering of severed arms.
They dangled from the rearview mirrors
and dropped along the road out of the canyon,
up Hank's Grade to the deep ravine
Lute Johnson dreamed he'd fill.

What a circus of slithers his garden became,
by the end of week one Lute
alone on his back porch just after dusk,
all the near distance before him
a locust whine of rattles, the contract good
for another nine hundred loads.
And before them all, the scouts and surveyors,
drillers and blasters, driving stakes
and locating benchmarks. They scoured
the untouched riverside, knowing
it would never be the same.
One blistering August afternoon a surveyor knelt
in the shade of a cottonwood grove
and sipped from a smooth basin
the clear spill from Pine Creek, so cold
it numbed his teeth and made his temples pound.
An hour's nap in long grass
left him plagued with a pox of ticks
he rolled to get away from. Imagine him
kneeling there, the burble of Pine Creek
a delicate counterpoint to his whimpers,
then Pine Creek alone when he saw them,
an audience of rattlers coiled
each in a hand-sized bowl of moss and rock,
looking and licking his way.
Or consider slick Albert Charbonneau, one-time powder monkey
from the Silver Valley mines, throwing the switch
and hearing the deep thunk, feeling the ground pitch
then seeing all around him, part and whole,
a bloody rain of snakes.

6. *Deliverance*

The word for her, I know now, was *florid*,
flushed and loudly fashionable Mrs. Evy Weeks.

For years I believed conversation
embarrassed her, a sunrise reliable blush
boiling her rouge to the skin edge of blood.
Midday in summer, come to her door
for the one-dollar wage her dandelioned lawn
had earned me, I watched her pinch
from her deep, floral coin purse
the usual four quarters, her cat's-eye glasses
giving me back my waiting self,
her pedal pushers in gold lamé
or the skin-taut, furless spots of leopards.
Her flesh seethed crimson,
as though the dark cool air rushing out
from behind her blew from a bellows,
the cracked dusty porch a forge.
She called me "Bobby," the hated diminutive,
and bent toward me with the silver
just far enough the brink of her breasts
showed at the scooped neckline
and reddened in my gaze like miraculous tomatoes.
She was beautiful, I think, and drunk.
Every day at dusk her husband emerged
and eased his gargantuan Buick
from the backyard garage and waited
at the curb for her, then headed,
my mother told me, for the track.
Each week their trash can filled
with a glockenspiel of bottles.
By the time I was thirteen
our paths diverged—mine halting
but ascendant, hers certain decline.
Though there was that day, shamed
by my mother's nag, I'd put off her yard
long enough, and began a surly, mean-spirited mowing,
dicing paper cups and cardboard beer coasters
heedlessly, taking out the sad, swallowed pansies

with the weeds. The copperhead
was huge, thick as a man's forearm
and sprawled in the shade below a window.
I panicked. No other word for it. I screamed
like a baby and froze against the chalky clapboards
crying momma. Spiked heels gone,
her bare feet came palely into view
lean and muscled as a tree-climbing girl's.
Her left hand, bedecked in baubles,
dazzled the snake's eyes away
just as her right reached down,
took the tail, and in a single, brute
whiplash stroke sent a wave
through flesh and scales
that blew the fanged head off
with a gunshot report. Then she was kneeling
before me, stroking my arms
and asking me was I bit, was I bit,
and holding me to her, I see now,
just as though we were dancing:
her head on my shoulder,
and behind her the headless snake,
a helix of death throe coils
coming to rest in the just-cut, musky greens,
and her ear, in a fog of perfume,
only inches from my eyes, and red as a rose.

   7. Glossolalia

Long interlocked ribly abundance scale
scatter racketer of bead isinglass skin slough
slick back tuck of fang and spit
pit black waggle tongue strummer
air boil hiss and spin all din and kingly silence
Lord and belly-slither symbol O snake.

Rake ravaged hoed up buried in air
and blasphemed blackberry transits cartilaginous
coil and sleepless swallower of mouse
you peristaltic simpleton pure and perfect
pig feed demon O snake O angel.

Cottonmouth dirt phallus prey
of hawk and owl first mind fuck
and venerable venomous original kin
sin slinging charmed tumescent skin bone
speed of blood needy foil and oil
slick agent of doom snake man mask of God.

8. *Paradise*

But O you nefarious marionettes, limbless,
slithering brethren, and mouthpiece
Howdy Doodies of Hell—consider
the greater burden of
omniscience, that cold-blooded certainty
of absolute foreknowledge, the way
the Lord saith, knowing full well all
He will have said, knowing full well
all He will have known. When the poet wrote
he'd sooner kill a man than a hawk,
I was not yet born, though I was well along
into my fifth decade when I saw
for the first time a hawk fly
over with a snake wriggling
in its talons. So plentiful the snakes here,
so plentiful the hawks, I hardly looked up
anymore, when a shadow caught my eye,
but did the day the hawk let go,
the snake in sudden spinning free fall,

my two youngest children at play in the yard.
Can you understand, Brother Snake, my swiftness,
all the old center fielder's instincts returned
as I leaped up and snatched the spade
from its spot beside the pumphouse and ran,
the shovel on its down-swing falling
only seconds after the serpent hit the ground,
not a dozen feet from where they played.
Some days, in high summer,
when just enough shade develops midday,
I can almost imagine the river below my house
the Euphrates, not the Clearwater,
and upstream, at the headwaters,
where the Selway spills from the wilderness,
a paradise, for all our doomed longing,
we've made a kind of park from,
where no one lives but the beasts
of field and forest, and all along
the sun-warmed canyons, your kind—
there, where I promise always
to leave you in peace.

9. *Resurrection*

The vast basaltic flows cooled to columns
or twisted half-set to a litter
of flagstones and cartoon wheels,
the earth today honeycombed
with caves and gaps, subterranean chambers
immune to seasons. All the better
for field mice and shrews, packrats
and meadow voles, rockchucks, ground
squirrels and moles, a vast scampering
cornucopia for the snakes. In spring

a green wash overwhelms the world,
and sprawled among the daffodils
a gartersnake tinged, chameleon in the leaves;
or as late as Thanksgiving, lacking the first
true frost, the dry grass crackle and clatter
of falling seed may still unnerve,
the last bumbling grasshoppers loosing
a racket to make the blood go cold.
But never in winter. Snowed over, the canyon's
at last traversible, the only perils
sheer depth or snow-hidden trip wires—
fallen fences, a blackberry's creeping vines.
So this is fabulous, a sweet trick of fate,
a frigid day in February and a full-grown rattlesnake
curled to a comma in the middle of the just-plowed road.
Ice ghost, I think, curve of rock
or stubbed-off branch. But the diamonds
are there, under a dust of crystals looming,
impossible, summer's tattoo, the mythical argyle of evil.
With the toe of my boot I nudge it.
Snow in the pasture is two feet deep,
a thermometer on the shed reads minus eight.
Mean leather, demon sap, I cannot
believe my eyes, my hands, and swing
the thing before me—snake saber,
venomous sickle, reptilian boomerang of ice.
There's nobody home but the dog
and me. She nips at the tail
and dances. If I threw this curved serpent
across the yard, she'd fetch it,
but instead I stuff it in a heavy burlap sack,
cinch the end tight with twine,
take it in the house and arrange it on the hearth.
Here's a cup of rosehip tea, a vodka snowshoe,
a cigar. Here are my wet gloves

dangling from their nails, holding nothing but air
in the shape of a thing—shaft, handle,
cylinder, smoke. Now the dog's asleep
in a parallelogram of sun, and one by one
a cold scent lures the cats from their lairs,
ears half-cocked. They sniff, they pat.
One hooks a claw in the woof or the warp
and pulls just enough to topple the sack
from hearth to carpet nap and jumps back
at the dim clack-clack inside.
Low in her throat, the dog rumbles—creak
of stone, light fall.
Call it Sunday, a day of rest.
I blow a huge, undulant ring of smoke
and wait.

Part Four

Night Music

1

The bass drum ka-thumps, the snare's a wire
live with cracks. It lacks a rasp of its own,
lightning unstrung in the formless air.
And the bell of the horn? Who can bear
its nightly burden, its blood pangs
and the breath of angels falling?
Sky is not lovely without a light,
though just as the melody gives way
to silence, the body implies the soul,
singing the notes all around it.
Now dreary autumns of eternity go by,
miles of filings. Leaf by leaf, the tree
turns a minor key, its song gone back to soil.

I hear the sidemen of water over stones,
the skeletal chords of night bird cymbals.
Along this mountain road, the wheels
of the wrecked truck spin on toward stillness,
the driver's undone but lucky, kneeling
and sick in the ditch. Deaf, the gray sky glowers
and smokes, the truck leaned
at such an angle I barely dare to move.
Posts uprooted, guardrail swayed out,
pulled tight as a string. I pluck it,
and for a mile the canyon fills
with a single, resonant, churchly note.
The world's afloat. No God is an island
in a sea of sins. The waves go on singing their way,
their way, the waves go on singing their way.

*

Things without voices, rejoice, rejoice;
things without hands take hands.
The tune's the illusion, the horn breathes
its eminent brass into gold. From the body
of earth, the swirl of wood, the soundboard hole
in the canyon air, it rises. I am,
it sang; I was, it sings; someone else
will be who will be.

2

Querulous, the magpie asks, "Aag-aag?"
Noise bag, contrapuntal cacophone, yes-man
of the nightly apocalypse. "Song," says the field
guide, lying. Likewise, the raven, papal
in his iridescent finery, regalia
of the unlapsed academic, going on and on without cause.
The song by God must embody all,
the whole scale, from baleful bawl
to twitter and giggle, love grunt and come cry,
gasp of dusk and sigh of dawn.
Who can imagine the painterly equivalent of Beethoven?
Some nights, in the deep, inhuman hills,
stars themselves go chiming.
In the pillow a blood-rush hisses,
rivets in a pan of spun brass.

Galvanized, the guardrail lit the truck lights up,
the driver looked but could not breathe.
All the needles of the larches, grown gold
with the cold, came shimmering down,
brush and stir. Drum put its ear
to the ground, the road itself took to humming.

Lively with leaping fish, the river grew.
What light was left was an aria. And eight slid-down steps
at a time, that one note vanished,
perking the worms, loosening the sockets
of mud-swaddled rocks, combing the hairs
of timbers and roots. Blind with eyes,
I could not hear the earthly riffs
and improvisations. I could not
see the harmony of its fears—that no one
would listen, that someone would hear.

Magpies jangled, the river poured on,
gradually water turned water again. Distant night birds
dithered and chirped. The whole note dome
of the dark came down, a passing
draft of exquisite music. A cappella night,
bow-skrick of cricket. Death rattle, black song,
a thousand solo requia per mile.
Inside my car, dashlights made a cloud of blue.
From the tape player, a horn
nuzzling the windows, needing the dark
far more than me or any man.

3

The locust's yellow leaf kiting down:
by last light, by glint of star off the car's silver skin,
it sank, neither love nor loss nor sign.
Down the wine-dark river
I drove away. Body, remember
that singing; hillside, recall that cry.
I am cupped and capsuled, swallowed
by the night inside the night. I want
the dead man playing in the spheres of woods

and water. I want the thing that lives
inside me out, aloft, borne up
and glistening, in a cape of rain.

Call the thing an owl. It's caught a raven,
sleepy, off the spar of a cedar snag,
the prey's black wings akimbo,
loud beneath the deadly skewer. They're a shadow
in the headlights, road unwinding to road
like a clock. Dear Lord, Coltrane's crying,
"Hear me out! Hear me out!," a spot-lit illusion,
his horn sending flesh
to the sky, into the nightclub fog, into the night,
where a deep river sets its own music off,
into the passing afterlife of air.

Ice Fishing

From open water at the lake's
unfrozen outlet, steam rises, a scrim
dim enough to turn the sun as round as a dime,

though it's still so bright across snow,
so low in the sky it rings
with a ball-peen clang behind his eyes,

each time he looks up
from his augered hole in the ice.
Wind spins a spider-silk filament

of frost from the dorsal fin of a quick frozen
blueback, and blood spots
the snow around the hole.

From the darkening woods
two coyotes pipe and prate, the late
mouse they toss aloft in play, the same

they'll squabble over soon. And soon
the sun will sink an edge in the ridge,
and the wind will chase its tail

behind the trees. Then the man will stand
and take his stool and the tool
for the ice and the tool

for the fish and the fish and leave.
Only the low, late coals of his fire left behind,
pinkening down toward pure black ash,

*

the hole scabbing over already with ice,
where the dark below blows a kiss to night,
by the blood-freckled cheek of the evening snow.

Prey

We're walking through stubble and rain—
hammered grasses, the dog and I. It's almost dawn,
almost December, the western ridge is lipped
with snow and catches early sun.
The canyon still deepens to the river's black sheen.
A rooster pheasant comes up,
gray receding dot going down. From the place
she'd trailed it to, the dog looks back.
There's a wraith of ground fog between us
but it's plain she's puzzled, put out.
"Out of season, girl," I shrug, "No gun."

Such is the curse of the single-minded. She'd
hound a bird broken-winged but still running
for half a mile through burdock and bramble,
into thickets of poison ivy, over roads
and fence rows, only to bring it back alive
enough to kick at my pale hand
headed for its neck. And my daughter,
who will not eat meat and loves the dog beyond all reason
cannot accept my answer
when she asks, "If we were starving,
would you kill Violet for food?"

Imagine night come down. It is winter, far
from any city or town. I stroke my daughter's back,
the dog sleeps alongside her bed. There is a God,
I think, and the bird that rises is His bauble,
and the dog duly and daily serves Him,
as we make our way from dark to dark,
His meat, as the sun that rises is His fire.

More Rain

—an elegy

Indolent and watery, the nightcrawlers sprawl
four or five a stride, all the way
to the mailbox. The robin on top's a bleary orb,
a rumpled bird ball fat with reprobation,
burdened out of flight by the realm's false coin.

Nothing but wet fliers from the better life,
nothing but bills, advertisements lurid with bait.
Here's a card from my sister, where the water's not
fit to drink; here's a catalog featuring
a million dollar bra. Licking the pages

will quench a thirst. And the robin, so fat
he cannot rise when I approach,
coasts down to the mud of the road.
There the worm meat's strung for miles,
and nearby the sated cat, having neither conscience
nor appetite, maintains its vigilant wait.

The trick, they say, is in loving the rain,
the ghastly abundance of open-mouthed flowers.
Some of the worms shine and swell—pink
seductive curls. They want it,
slurs the bird, and the ground fog whispers, So do I.
Now the red flag has fallen, now the thin door has closed.

As for the cat, it was all sometimes too much for him:
a mate's scent and everywhere a clatter of drops,
the supple and too silent transits green weeds provide for vermin.

He sniffs a worm and looks up perplexed, a tuffet
of down in his whiskers, having mistaken something else entirely
for the sound of rain on the road.

Peace

—for Judy Blunt

Like the minutes of a board meeting
or the recitation of guidelines that pertain,
the dull, unembellished piano went on,
each verse another course of bricks.
Under other circumstances, such playing
might have walled us off from the melody,
especially this one, "Silent Night,"
swaddled as it is in ponderous reverence
and a contortionist's inversions in the service
of rhyme. But we were parents and grand-
parents, watching in ranks along the gymnasium's wall
our two hundred children and children's children
not sing at all but sign, hands
and arms fluttering, four hundred pale wrens
tethered to their souls.
              But it is not
Christmas; it is spring, April, 1995,
and I am trying to explain to my daughter
the front page pictures that have made me cry.
She is frightened of audiences, not catastrophe.
Her hands as she struggled at Christmas to save her place,
as she flushed redder every chorus,
sailed milliseconds before or after
that spot the pianist pounded out for words.

Months later my explanations do likewise:
for the baby's bloodied head,
for the woman's nowhere eyes
neither of us can stop seeing—
the arc of rebar across her, the leg

they will amputate to set her free,
her mother, her baby, her three-year-old child
nowhere to be found.
                              People like us,
I say, everyone is people like us.
And did I mean by that, when I sent her
off to school this morning, a kind
of parental lie? Some of us,
I believe, *are* different,
and what comes back to me then
is that droning, flourishless piano,
how it took us calmly and clearly
to where, at the end of the song,
at its final refrain, we could see:
four hundred hands upraised
and fluttering the penultimate modifier,
"heavenly," then falling to their chests,
cradles of skin and bone at the ribs, cages
of bone for the hearts, beating on
as though it were still possible to believe
in the last word.

Arrowhead

—for Dennis Held

A century of recent sand washed away
by flood, and so this trinket,
this flint shrapnel glistening on the beach at Agatha.
Among the trailer house calamities,
the river-twisted corrugated roofs
of a dozen sheds and stables,
this delicate point the color of caramel.

For the hooded merganser, perhaps,
in hard enough times, or the succulent forest grouse
gullibly drumming, or the fine toothsome flesh
of a migrating Canada goose, basking
in the shallows. He might have sat there himself,
the man who made it, on that flat-topped rock
an arm's length upstream, where the wet season

side-creek spills and the chunks of quartz
gleam among the common clinkers
like faces in a crowd of gray.
Every worked fleck and chip (there are tons
all down the river) speaks of meat,
but still, now and then, a whole one,
like this, lost, cast off, or abandoned.

Or else borne by the goose it killed
to the rapid edge of the current and washed
to just this place, or carried here
in the jaws of the lucky coyote,
to nestle in the long rot of sand
until the recent flood, and then me.
Or rather, not me, but my friend,

*

for whom the points and spear tips shine,
whose eyes by flint light
can sift among the bottomless trove of common
rounded stones, and who smiled
and bent down and plucked this very one up
from the sand between my dull toes
and made of it his gift to me.

Imagine that instant of almost silence,
only the river's constant wash
as the arrowhead finds its home.
I am the one who lives here,
and the load of ore upended by my hand
might stem river's flow, though
in all my hopeful turnings

I have never found an arrowhead myself.
Pity the hunter come home empty-handed,
the hours at work with a hammer
of elk horn, an obsidian awl, and all gone
for naught. Little death messenger,
may the meat you made have fed him too,
from his brother's spit the skin-crackling

goose flesh buttery with oils and smoke.
Imagine too that moment between two men,
my friend and me, one hopeless
hunter and gatherer, the other
unhanding his embarrassment of riches.
Once, in a single afternoon,
my friend found three perfect points,

three impeccable, serrate blades,
each a hand-span from the next

and in sight of my living room window.
Then the chill at his neck came down—
call it white man's mojo, some meaning
too deep, a lost language chiseled in stone.
I was the one not far upstream,

kneeling, in search of something
whole, in the catholic posture of prayer,
as he cupped them in his palm,
closed his eyes, and let them fly
back to the ancient river. This made thing, then,
from one man to another. We keep looking,
though I have more than I will ever need.

Nostalgia

Verily, my wife grew round and gave birth,
and her breasts, those lovely baubles, became
mammary glands, lactate factories, unfirmed
unto womanliness and not a bit less lovely.
I was put out not so much
by four years of near monopoly
one child, then another, wrought
upon her chest—she was as generous
as she could bear to be—but by the bond
between her and those babies.

Bottle-fed myself, I felt a formal bow
accruing in the vicinity of my mother's buttons.
Always between us some membrane
of man-made cloth, my most powerful muscle,
the jaw, and the blood-deep mammalian impulse
to suck satisfied on a bland protuberance
of mass-produced rubber.
And I have tasted (I told you
she was generous) my wife's first oozings
of colostrum and known in my heart

I was the interloper there, stranger
if not to the child just then too sleepy
to nurse, then to the breast itself,
its ambrosial sap. My sad delectable pain.
No one loves the skin
of which I speak more than I.
The arduous weanings are long past,
I have gathered all my playthings unto me
repeatedly and made my fealty known:
I am possessed, inhabited. I am happily lost.

*

And I do not blame my mother. We were twins
then, my sister and I, in that postwar, techno-euphoria
responsible today for dead rivers
and nuclear havoc all across America.
I lived my first year on something
ominously and frankly called—even today—"formula."
But O children, all children, I miss it,
I miss it so: my youngest son used to rise
red-faced, eyes rolled back in his head,
and murmur, "Other side," then fall again,
to what I know I never knew.

Bodies

Too soon, the foreshadowed curves
come forth from my daughter's body. She is ten
and wanted this night to bathe alone,
thus breaking her little brother's heart.
Privacy and changes, a sermonette
of parental guidebook and buzzword blather:
I held his small body to me as he cried
himself to sleep. She curled up with a book
in her bed, pink and flushed with identity,
her mother having combed out her hair.

Let us mourn the advent of modesty, I say later on.
The dog looks up expectant, inquisitive.
She'd been licking herself with that rapt
intensity her breed is famous for,
and now, head aslant and tongue protruding,
she looks as foolish as I must look,
having sock-by-shirt-by-shorts stripped
to stand naked in the center of the room,
arms extended like a tenor awaiting his roses.

Everyone's asleep but the two of us,
and the dog's grown weary, what itch
or animal impulse to groom that afflicted her earlier
gone. Still, here I am, going
door to door, checking locks and turning out lights,
all but the one beside the easy chair
where I intend to sit and read the daily paper.
But first, I step out onto the porch
and the dog comes along. Our distant neighbors'
houses are dark, one solitary car plies its way

along the river road, and I remember
a night almost thirty years ago,
a girl and I drove the downtown streets
buck naked in my father's Mercury.
The car windows were nearly clear
of the fog our hours of parking brought on.

At first she giggled and I grinned,
but on the second or third pass down Main Street
we grew expansive and serious.
This was grown-up business, we were sure
of it. She no longer slouched
or slunk down in her seat at the stop signs.
Under the radio's blare, the tires thrummed,
and the air filled with our musk.
We stayed like that all the way
to her house, where she dressed herself
by dashlight, kissed me once on the lips
and let her hand slide down my nearly hairless chest.
What magic there was might have lasted
all night, if she had not left then,
if the dome light had not gone on
and shown me there behind the wheel,
a boy not so much naked anymore as peculiarly nude,
bare, even, pale and grinning.
She loved me, she loved me not, but could not
help herself and laughed before the door slammed.

The dog nuzzles at my hand. The strangeness
of human beings is nothing new to her,
so under the light I sit, exposing myself
to the news. The world
is a mess, horror and treachery abound.
The paper's bottom edge nests
against my ordinary, unweaponly cock.

War too is grown-up business, and money,
and the body as well, a concern and a currency,
powerful and weak, manipulative and manipulable.

In love with all he feels, my son sleeps.
In the weeks to come, despite his pleas
and wheedles, his elaborate bubble bath
and squirt gun seductions, he'll bathe alone.
We will call it growing up, the long
solitary journey every body makes,
through the neighborhoods of modesty
to the homeland of shame, to the vast
uncharted wilderness of desire. We will not say so,
but already he is left behind, blind
to his sister's sudden hips and new swellings,
the last human soul in the household
perfectly at ease without his clothes,
and the touch of skin on air and light.

Prayer for the Winter

I place two pennies, one on either rail:
warm from my pocket they melt the frost there
then harden into place against the coming tremors.

The ties too are tufted white, and fibrous mounds
of coyote scat, and the next occasional spike
worked loose, which I fling like the others in the river.

A crooked volunteer tree offers up its last
or its only apple, hard and thick-skinned,
bitter still but sweetened a bit by the cold.

Along this mile-long arc of track, four springs
and four steep chutes choked with blackberries,
and four cold pools crowded with cress.

It's a black fly wind, all ice and bite,
and the usual fishermen have all gone home.
Trainmen hate those pennies. I'll hide

until the engine's past, hide again
for the obsolete caboose this short-line throwback
still uses. They hate the clunk and jump,

the eighty-ton shudder pummeling their bones.
But I want something to show for this day
other than a mile of awkward walking,

a wind so fierce and relentless the chimney smokes
lie out in rigid lines and vanish and the only smell
is snow, snow, snow, like a fat and generous relative

coming all day but still too far off to see.
And when it arrives, the lead cloud billowy and black,
the first icy spits will sting like little fires.

Already the downstream train plows from under it
and rounds the corner flocked, a thunderous cake,
a mile of steel, a birth-water umbilicus

harkening storm, and I, who must ply
the deadman roads and walk the skin-tingling
right-of-way corridor, I don't ever want it to stop.

Not the train, not the snow, not the winterkill wind
that blows and blows. No, let it snow,
let the earth go blind and the highway unlined.

Let it come down like sleep, let the deep drifts
extend their leeward fingers and the springs spill
into long random sculptures of ice.

Wouldn't it be nice, marooned in a frozen world
for a night one long winter long, home
where the fire burns the years and wind

sings its one note wavery aria over and over,
and we are alive, alive, in a place
where nothing matters but that we are warm

where the children toss their gossamer
untenderable coins against the weather,
and never lose, and never, never lose.

Conjure

There is nothing of her body he can't
conjure—texture, heft, taste, or smell.
This is heaven, and this is also hell.
He can dream the way moonlight comes slant

through the window, illuminating breast
and breast, her navel a shadowy pool
he drinks the darkness from, her skin grown cool,
and her lips and her lips and all the rest.

If she were here, he thinks, and he thinks too
much, he thinks. He thinks too much when she's here,
and when she's gone. And the window's a mirror
he's all alone in. If he could say he knew

every night would be made of her, a thigh
in the true air, her long, elegant spine
blossoming forth from the clothes on the line,
he would have asked, he would have asked her why

the sigh of the evening breeze is her tongue
and the rose of her cast off shirt his hand
unfillable and trying. He can stand
and go and find her still-damp towel among

the morning's last mementos, and the shape
of her ear, a whorl on the pillow's white.
He can feel the whole weight of her at night
and the weight of her absence, and her hip.

He would say when she's gone he loves too much.
He's immoderate or reckless. He cries

and laughs at his crying, his dreams are lies
he cannot live without, a drunk, a lush,

inebriate of skin and tongue and hair.
But reason has no mouth to kiss, no eyes
he dives in. His head aches. He is not wise,
but strokes the round, blue corporeal air

and conjures her painfully into place.
Most chaste of lovers he is, a shadow
man enamored of another shadow,
and the dark he is kissing is her face.

Envoy

The Name

1

The end of it, the start, a heart speck
flickering in the ultrasound. Around and around it
the smear of flesh, swirl of home,
a shadow, the spirit's limber bones building.
I slept on my back for years not to hear—
in my ear, some god in his robes contouring
the slope of a dune. He would come for me. I was doomed,
and I knew it. What feeble engine is this?
Ignition, parturition, pairs of arms and eyes,
all that delicate, permeable skin. You're in,
and that's the sin, all the rest is dying.

So they say, little cloud man, wing light pulse
in the sonographic sky. Why deny it?
The end's assured, irrefutable, and maybe not
an end at all. The call of your heartbeat
takes me deeper. I've been napping so long
the whole vast expanse of me tingles,
I'm dazzled by knives, by the waves
set loose in your mother's round house.
How's about a name for you, boy? a face?
a fate? Something to need, perhaps, above all else,
some pall that implies the brightest light,
a skin to love even more than your own.

Here is the dark and here is the day.
Where you live for now—in the gray wash
of waves, an inland sea and barrage of noise—
is all on earth you will ever know

of perfection. Gill-slits gone, fins
uncoiling toward a grasp, the genital array
lapsed to the single curse and election.
Your sister's more beautiful than all the stars.
You are strong and free for the incremental march,
until you bury me.

2

Cottonwood, cottonwood, let down your fluff.
The nests abound, plush as lactating breasts.
Clutches of eggs, all the thicket's adorned,
a hundred sacks of twig and grass.
In the spring duff, cottonwood, your root-sucker
others come greening into place,
the uprights and shoots. What an ecstasy
of fumbling the bees in your blossoms bring on.
A pygmy owl's knothole hoos
above my head, the rounds of branches
wound my instep and arch. It's March.
Bud resin musk coats the skin of the sky.

Here's an ear hump, a bass clef
mirrored and turned childish heart.
Now I'm carving initials
so far up the trunk, only birds and rain
will read them. I celebrate
impermanence, I personify the fire that is faith.
Blunt, pulpy wood, smooth bark
scarified by my hand, let this tattoo leak
down the cambium shaft come autumn,
let its birthmark enter the veins
and emerge, blood-sap and dream of leaf,
into the born and born and yet unborn.

*

My hair grows wisps, the catkins' shed froth.
Pitch gloves my hands with dust.
I have married a tree in the gold
spring sun, I have stated my love with a blade.
Cottonwood, cottonwood, let me down slow.
You know how the earth awaits us, my eyes
the color of somewhere loam. I am damned,
it's true, but holding on, darned to the tree
by the looped light threads all flights of sparrows
pull along. I believe if I fall
I will not fall far.

3

Bud, then blossom; root, then tree.
The sap pulse of syringa, sun scope
pendulum, half the earth turning to watch. Swollen,
the labia stretch, the lips then the lips,
a swatch of scalp
and the arduous birth gush begins.
It's lush, a wonder, the redolent waters
spinning us aswim in amniotic air.
From the womb of the hills and fields and forest,
from flesh of dirt and furrow of flesh,
a boy grows forth and lets fly his limbs
and swims again in the tragedy of air.
Where will he go? What will he pray to?
The latch at the breast is sweet beyond whiskey.
Colostrum's rich. They are blossom to blossom,
they are petals and pinks. The stink
of my sweat tinctures his breathing.

Little boy, little man, it's in you too,
current and spark, parent and parent and child.

Your delicate scapulas pump, the wings
of the circuit stroke the soul into being.
Cry and cry, tiny fossicker. You fidget,
the nut meats of your fists open out into hands—
calyx and fingerprint, contours of the earthly whorls.
All the worlds revolve in your name, revenant drum
in the valley of the breasts, and like the turn of the leaf,
like the sap's rise and fall, the fontanel springs,
a faithful code it receives and sends,
the word at last we all are known by,
where the cap of your animal hair pounds.

BARRY KOUGH

Robert Wrigley lives with his wife and children in the canyon of the Clearwater River in Idaho. His previous book, *In the Bank of Beautiful Sins*, won the San Francisco Poetry Center Book Award and was a finalist for the Lenore Marshall Award from the Academy of American Poets. He is also the recipient of two Pushcart Prizes, two National Endowment for the Arts grants, a fellowship from the John Simon Guggenheim Memorial Foundation, as well as the Frederick Bock, and J. Howard and Barbara M. J. Wood Prizes from *Poetry*.

PENGUIN POETS